The House
I'm Running From

Michelle M. Tokarczyk

West End Press

The author thanks the editors of the following publications in which some of these works first appeared:

Arts Focus, Conditions, The Dan River Anthology 1986, *Home Planet News, The Literary Review, the minnesota review, New Poets Anthology, Ormfaer, Scintillations II* and *Soundings*.

First edition — September 1989
ISBN 0-93112253-8

Typography by Prototype

West End Press
P.O. Box 27334
Albuquerque, NM 87125

Table of Contents

"They see me running for the White House.
They don't see the house I'm running from."

—Jesse Jackson
address to the
Democratic National Convention
Atlanta, Georgia, 7/20/88

The House I'm Running From

To the Safety Net

Names, numbers
flashed
on the blackboard
like
snowflakes
on a dark night
impossible
to clutch.

Each day I wrapped
a scarf
across my mouth,
headed through
the cold for home.
How many
ten-year-old steps?
How many
cracks of ice?
to the house
with no curtains
windows shaking
alone in the wind.
I said no
to the tag games,
the snowmen,
went to
the living room
warmed
with all the furnace
we could afford,
to the bed
in the warm room
with all
the blankets
we owned.

I didn't know
the sandwich
every day
would make me
better.

Didn't know
I pulled on
a weighted jumper
because
I'd pushed
supper meat
in guilty circles.
Didn't know
I'd decided
to not eat.

I knew only
mommy's hair
hung limp
with worry.
We were fed
early;
my parents
hid their plates
that seemed
too light;
my stomach
clamped
at the sight
of my meal.

And then
I took
long naps
and woke
to words
too weak
to answer.
How are you
feeling?
Daddy put
his hand on
my forehead.
How did I know?
I stayed home
from school,
watched a movie
about

an outlaw
hiding
in a swamp,
saw him sink
down, down
down into
quicksand.
I cried
for the hat
floating
on the top.

Evening came,
parents, sister
came, we knelt
clutching
rosary beads,
daddy leading
with sorrowful
mysteries.
Christ alone
crying:
Take this away!
Christ on display
crying:
It is finished
into thy hands
my spirit.

Prayers were over.
I curled in the far
corner of
the bed, knees
to the wall
blanket
to my chin,
towards
security
I couldn't
recall.

Heritage

At sixteen my grandmother
said good-bye to her parents, good-bye
to her siblings, good-bye to their farm,
good-bye for what she could not
admit was forever.
Got on a boat for America
to scrub out a living
and maybe, maybe
learn to read and write.

For weeks she coughed up salted food,
for weeks she stared into faces
of people without homes,
for weeks she was terrified
lice would burrow into
her braided scalp, be uncovered
by the inspector's pared fingers,
and she, exiled on an island,
doomed to watch the ocean foam.

Years later her two sons were drafted.
(Two had already died of whooping cough.
Their infant bodies could not be calmed
though her arms tried to squeeze
illness out of them.)
All she said was "not the navy."
For European land . . . if
it had to be . . . but she would not give
her children to that water.

When she went into the nursing home,
she couldn't wash her hair, still couldn't
sign her name. In the home she drooped
on the bed they made; tried
to talk to nurses whose eyes
never shifted with her stories.

We have landed rockets on the moon.
Men chop off chunks of satellites.
Their bodies float in space.
Why would we care about oceans?

After Woyko's Disappearance

Grandma walked
the same parks
the same streets
every day,
the pain
as constant
as the concrete,
the bottle
as constant
as the pain
until there were
bouts of darkness
stretching over
days of concrete.

At twenty-two
I envisioned
hope in
stretched-thin skin,
yanked a bottle
from wrung-out hands,
even said
"I want you
to be happy"
to ears babushka-sealed,
eyes turned toward
the lost brother
the dead husband,
head shaking no
to these days.

In my new apartment
I pulled down the shades,
watched the darkness
with a whiskey bottle.

Granny's Death

There comes a time
when your veins
constrict blood,
toes crumble
weary of walking,
body sagging
with memory.

First bound
to an old age home
then bound
to a hospital bed,
you pray;
they plan
to chop off
one limb
at a time.

Plastic nourishment
pumps through
your veins;
a few teeth
are all
you have left
and all you need
to sever it.

Parochial Child

Not allowed
to wear a winter coat
in the bishop's parade—
it would hide the school colors,
camouflage the faith—
she sat in the
outdoor stadium
rubbing gloved hands
over bumpy flesh
blowing cold breaths through
prayers to faithful martyrs,
teeth chattering to
the march of blocked plaids.

Five years later
she sneaks 'round the corner
of the convent after
fall exams; sucks nicotine
with chapped red lips; hikes
her skirt in defiance.

Work Clothes

You classify the clothing
by the way the eyes meet it;
come up against a slate
of blue pinstripe, try
to absorb it; resist
the impulse to lick
your lips at gray flannel,
ponder its soft undertones;
is there anything there for you?

My father the parkie wore a sour
green uniform; eyes butted
past him like receptacles he filled.
At age five I went with him to work.
His back filled the width of his shirt;
his hand folded around mine;
my little legs hurried
to get there on time.

At the park I helped spear papers,
stared at the deep green of blunted grass
and the chain link fence around us.

Unemployed

In the morning
I'll wake up;
wash last night's
bad dreams
from my face;
set my place
with coffee
the classifieds
my five-act play;
resolve to
begin again;
remembering
school's begun again.
I'll be back next year
or the year after—
I'll be back after
this is over;
I'll begin again.
Remembering
my teeth hurt;
can't drink hot liquids
right away.
the rent is due;
the month begins again.
Tear the ads in half
push aside the play:
the coffee has the day.

Lunchtime in the Garment District

The cold stops
breath in your throat
padded shoulders sag
as your body sinks.

Gloved hands crawl
out of recycled mutton
lining frayed
as hours upstairs
punching out
another's profits.

Pull together
two ends of hide:
The wind is yours
for half an hour.

A Favor

There were too many years
when I'd walk from bars
unsteadily to street lamps
on a block I'd recognize
as mine.

But this was one night:

I reached for my key,
found him at my side.
I didn't know why.
He came in, even held me
as I cried.

I went to lie down. He
stretched beside me
on too narrow a couch.
I threw up. He cleaned up,
returned, unbuttoned my
blouse,
unzipped my pants. I said no—
I'd get pregnant.
He put my hand on his cock.
I said I was too tired.
He said it wouldn't take long.
(I guess it didn't.)

When he left he copied
my number off the phone.
When he called he reminded me
he'd cleaned up.

Discerning Rapists

Gauge veins pulsing
in a mass of arm,
voice rippling
compliments,
eyes probing . . .
what?

Will he scrape me
off in layers?
Think I'm Charlie Tuna
itching to be snared
by the finest?
Grateful for the knife
at the throat,
the gashes
in very private parts,
the grace
of tin-can packaging?

Gauge eyes
fixing too long
on hips shifting away;
eyes following
through deepening night
through swirls of rain;
hands offering
umbrella shelter
I grasp without knowing.

An Alternate Ending to a Temp Job

Contributors' Notes

Michelle M. Tokarczyk is a poet, critic and assistant professor who has published in numerous journals. She was born and raised in a working-class family in New York City. She received her B.A. from Herbert Lehman College and her Ph.D. from SUNY at Stony Brook. Before completing her education, she held a variety of temporary clerical positions.

Her Co-worker Talks

I'm still trying to put it all together.
From what I hear she was just down on her luck.
She was trying to get an advanced degree
but didn't have
a lot of money or confidence in herself.
She'd been too nervous and too broke to do her work,
so she left school to get a full-time job and finish
at night. After looking for work for a few
weeks and finding nothing, she was getting scared.
I guess a friend told her about this place,
a temp job collating papers at this warehouse
on the west side of Manhattan. It was one of those
old buildings with windows that always shook
when you stepped down too hard, windows so caked
with grime and soot it always seemed dark outside.
Her friend told her sure, it was a shit job,
but if she just took it for a few weeks she'd
get Unemployment and be o.k. . . .
Yeah, I needed money too, needed money bad.
Why else would anyone work there?

Right after we got there we heard about a lot
of crimes in the neighborhood. A lot of drugs,
a lot of pimping on the street. But like I said
we all needed money, and you always tell yourself
you'll be all right.

I didn't know what to think about her.
She was what, 24? Well, she looked a lot younger.
With that hair she cut herself, that baby face,
and God she was tiny! Every day she wore
overalls and carried a knapsack with a thermos
of coffee, lunch and *The Complete Milton* in it.
Can you beat that! . . . She seemed depressed.
Everybody in a place like that's depressed,
but she seemed like she really had something
on her mind. . . . Lunchtime she'd go back
to the loading dock where it was really quiet
and read that Milton. Said she was working
on a paper or something. Was trying
to get some money together (on that salary!)
and go back to school. I'd invite her
to eat lunch with me, or go out for a walk,
get away from the dust. It was early September,
still sunny and warm. You could feel
like a human being just walking down 14th Street,
maybe buying some cheap blouse
you'd probably never wear. But no, she'd
just sit on that unused loading dock,
drinking that dank instant coffee and eating
American Cheese, and doing whatever
she was doing with that book and a lot of notes.

That's where it happened.
Two guys shot her, execution style.
They took her just inside the loading area,
told her to lie down and fired three bullets
into her head. Police say the motive's
robbery, but I don't know about that.
She was so little, and it doesn't look
like she struggled. She probably would've
given them everything she had.
Why'd they have to kill her?

. . . I don't think she was involved in drugs.
You never can tell, but she didn't seem like the type.
They didn't rape her or do anything like that . . .
I always think men will do those things,
but the police don't find any evidence they did.
I can't figure it out.

I don't know what she was doing, but I keep thinking
about how she wanted to go back to school.
All those notes she was scribbling for some kind
of work. I don't know why it was so important to her;
it sure wasn't worth her life. . . .
She was a nice kid though. Wish I'd gotten
to know her better, but that's it . . .
she didn't talk much.

Leaving the Subway, Approached by a Pornographer

It was not
pants tightened
in shrinking,
tongue nervously
tracing lips.

It was my hair
too fine,
falling in wisps
across my face.
My eyes
too tired,
sinking into
dark circles.

And, small
to begin with
my shoulders
crouching into
my chest.

So little
space around me
and other people
filling it all.

Malice

I

It takes years to learn a city.

Arms sway back and forth,
traffic stops, speeds,
eyes dart at shadows
on good blocks and bad.

The small town girl
sips soda in bars;
learns the best way
to evade eyes,
the safe stride,
the body that does not
sway with the breeze.

But even then
there's one mistake.

She thought she'd won.
The landlord promised
to give her own money
back to her.
So she went
just outside the bar
where the heat
sticks to the darkness,
where the landlord's
lifetime buddies
wait with razors.

One man straddles her
heart, that pounds loud
as the helplessness
of her screams
drenched in blood,
while the other slashes
through her flesh,
straight through
the muscles
in the model's face,
slashes, cuts
gaping gashes
100 sutures
healing into scars
medically assessed
"basically permanent."

II

Only a makeup artist
could slash like that.

Only the fingers
that contoured cheekbones
sharpened shadows
above the eyes,
camouflaged shadows below.

Only those hands could gash
across one cheek, down the other
slice a network
around the eyes
that could not open
wide enough to absorb
the face fixed
on hacking to her teeth.

"Well Tonight Thank God It's Them Instead of You"

I

Your hair to the shoulders
will not wave;
polyester flowers fade
in another soaking.
Coffee hours old
in the thermos
aches your shoulder.
Blunted heels click
to classified ads
agency blocks. Jobs
crossed out one by one.

Find your spot
in Welfare.
You are different from
all the other spots—
younger, brighter, whiter.
Present your resources:
empty bankbook,
cum laude B.A.
Clutch your arms
across your breasts
that heave knowing
eyes assess
tight flesh, face yet
unlined; eyes comb
terminal stations
for eyes you can
no longer hide.

Remember your difference
as you grope
for bottles
under sweat-soaked bed.
Limbs ache awake without work.

The cabinet opens
to a jar of rice;
the mailbox opens
to no check.
The cabinet opens
to an empty jar,
slams to the hands
blocking tears
from cracked walls.

II

But this year
December's wind
will not crack
the corners of your eyes.

This year's slush
will not seep
into your feet.

You will run
with a white silk dress
shielded in plastic
past a ragged woman
feet wrapped in plastic

as she calls
"Hey, watch it, watch it . . .
your dress is draggin'
gettin' dirty."

Acknowledgments

To everyone who helped me become
a woman who could get a Ph.D.

To Free Therapy for College Students

I underlined words
in a student handbook,
"psychological counseling,"
"personal problems."
Five or six months
I walked the halls
my eyes tracing
his bold name
on the office door.
Finally I slumped
into a chair,
a childhood crying
in lonely hallways;
hands squeezing arms
fighting back words
until . . .
My voice, at first
so strange, I
recognized—
grew to like
my inflection
the pitch of my words.
Over years my arms
stretched across the chair.

To Legalized Abortion

It was too hot in the South Bronx;
I took off his denim jacket,
felt the width of his shoulders
in my hands.
My legs stretched out tan.
My hands though trembling traced
every line of his body.
Days itching
in plaid skirts, wool blazers.
Nights of my restless hands
on my cloth nightgown,
praying to the open arms
of a dead god.
At twenty I opened
my mouth to his.

In one month
there was only one spot
of blood on my panties.
In the South Bronx
there are rooms
of women, at twenty
children latched to hands
backs against the stoop
eyes halting
at the stoop
across the street.

In a white room
in a white paper gown
they bled me red.
At twenty I sat
recovering, turning
my eyes toward the horizon
I could not see.

An Academic Fantasy

I still have hope
that one day after,
please, not too many more
years of teaching all day
writing all night
I'll get that job.

And after
seven more years
multiplied by how many
aspirin, how many valium,
how many exhausted arguments,
wavering between crying and
screaming, hugging and
hating my husband—
or how many years alone
my drooping head propped
in my own iced hands—

After all these years
I'll get tenure,
I'll never drink another
cup of coffee. Never eat
dried cheese while running
down the street.
My body will sway
in the freedom of daily
jazz classes. I'll lie
in a chair, feel the sun's
rays warm my eyelids to resting.

I'll have my own money,
my own health insured,
my own title will inscribe
my own office door.
I'll fill my shelves
with dusted books.

That childhood crying unheated
under an old winter coat of
        a blanket,
closing my eyes to the muffled
sounds of my mother's cries,
that childhood, those years
        expiated.
They'll see it, point to me
dream of me, the American Dream.

And I will tell them no, no.
I will tell them dreams
        require sleep.

American Images

I

In Jamaica the sunlight
eased into my body,
the warmth soaked out my pores;
the green was so thick
to my city eyes, so bent
to its own shape, full
of its own sounds:
I called it magical.

In Jamaica Steve's outstretched
arms grip the edge of the bar
he tends. His head bends toward
the rum-soaked wood as he speaks
through rotting teeth:
"I want to go to America."
A dream swallowing his eyes,
pulsing from his wrists
to his shoulders. Every day
on a two-hour, forty-mile bus ride
at every jagged blinding turn
he sees an image of iced water
peeking around Lady Liberty.

II

At sixteen my grandmother came to America
to scrub out a living, and maybe, maybe
learn to read and write.
When I was sixteen my mother told me
I would have to leave school,
get down on my hands and knees,
scrub floors. I thought no I'll do that
for no one, but if I must, I'll go to
school all night long.

I never did scrub floors, but I've spent
my time choking on the garment district's dust
watching my hands as collating machines.

That was a long time ago.
Before I spent years of nights and days
marking my words in margins of texts.
I will never go hungry now. No more,
I'm sure, will I huddle in doorways,
eating hardened cheese and dried bread,
breaking from a minimum wage job. Still,

my eyes begin to burn with printed pages;
veins around them break in strain,
my throat tightens at night as
I gulp caffeine, scour papers till
the evening chill stretches into morning.

At thirty-five I reread job lists, circle
possibilities, a chance (just a chance)
for permanent work, just a chance,
just some time for my own writing.

I could see myself in a tenure-track
line. I could see myself being granted
tenure. I would look as I do now.
But I would not constantly tap my fingers.
I would not stride with such quick, wide steps
or suck my fingers against my mouth.
I tell myself that's all. The person
who can have tenure looks back
in the mirror with darker green
eyes than her grandma's. She has your
words, you can put her in job letters.
That's what I tell myself.

Working into Night

Reading my writing after writing all day,
my neck, shoulders slacken;
I push my fingers into my temples,
feel the pulse of my blood
while chiseling a paper
for MLA, for San Francisco,
for the state with the fault line
jagging into its earth.

Sometimes as I sit quietly my heart
doubles its pace, the result
I've been told of a defective valve
prolapsing, refusing to seal
as it pumps blood.

I might sit here as blood cakes
around my heart; a displaced, renegade
platelet lodges itself in a vessel.
I might lose control of one arm,
peripheral vision in one eye,
or have a major stroke and lose
everything I know as me.

I've seen pictures of the fault line;
the two plates shifting, trembling,
setting off periodic shocks measured
by seismographic waves, by changes
in the behavior of cats, by the
fluctuations of the moon.

There are labs of people studying
the earthquake; they know its patterns,
its fault line veins, approximate
its force on a scale; they know
everything but when it will strike.

In San Francisco there's a woman
going to the MLA; she'll get on BART,
jot down busy notes as the train
rushes through the tunnel under the bay,
and she jots down busy notes till the shaking
begins below the earth, till water rushes in.

My heart beats to the speed of the words
I read aloud from the paper I present
at San Francisco
while leaning forward in a folding chair
tapping my foot on the solid floor.

A Woman Writing in America

People tell me I'm lucky
my husband makes real money.
I know I am.

How many days
I went out
looking for work.
The summer sun,
an unrelenting spectator,
glared above me
as each block resounded
in those heeled pumps
or the winter froze
blood in my lips.
I could not wrap
a scarf tight enough
against a throat
swallowing hard.

How many days
I hoped to exhaust
the streets for
a little more money.
Most of the time
the streets won.
How many days
I went home
to blank walls,
blank splintered floors,
blank sheets pulled over
the cot, blank paper
at the typewriter.
My eyes closed, my mind
burrowed under my pillow.

There may have been
rich material,
powerful images here.
But they soaked away
in sweaty nightmares.

In my own office
filled with heat or
cooled air, where
I can press my toes
into the carpeting,
writing's easier.
I can pick for words
like pens. Can face
a blank with images
I'm not terrified
to conjure.

But when
we applied to buy
this home, I knew
I'd applied to buy
what my salary, my
history could
never buy.

At the interview
I sat till
the building sponsor
turned to me: "And do
you intend to work? . . .
O, you do work . . .
You write . . .
You teach English . . .
I barely speak that."

Being Middle Class

Sweat will always
bead like blood.
Suits will always stick
to a subway body
slackened by
desks and deadlines.

I will always wait,
thinking of the right
thing to say.
Anything but what I want to say:
You don't have
to go back.

The walls still hold
the winter's cold.
Street voices beg
spare change.
I shut the door
behind them.

Because I cannot
say those words
I will always say
the wrong thing.
We will spend
our evenings
locked in the silence
of our home.

A Night of Insomnia after Days of Arguing with My Spouse

Insecurities pulse
through my veins,
tensing my limbs,
rolling my head
over and over,
till finally
they wake me up,
keep me up,
as he sleeps
with his back
turned beside me.

In the morning
I go away
to work for
a few days.
The knapsack
weighs heavily
on my back
as I get on
the commuter train.

Too dazed to read
too restless to sleep
I gaze at
the landscape
of silent homes
in pastel colors
dotting drying grass.
Skeleton branches
crack across my window:
I tell myself it's autumn;
that's all.

Fragments toward Recovery

I

There are days when yet
I cannot trace
my fingers down his spine
without feeling again
how my slurred words
racked him.

II

At Cancun the ocean
rinses my sweat,
its warmth startles
like aqua waves
I meet to the knees
knowing of
the undertow
that could pull me out
beyond all reach—
especially
since I can't swim
since my body sinks
like the night.

III

Doug, your fingers
tightening around
your wife's throat—
the darkness of
the moment you sealed
off her air;
the darkness of
the third time down.
At twelve I almost drowned.
My lungs lost all their air;
I collapsed in the water.
The darkness of nights
emptying bottles,

the darkness of mornings
reading my crimes in eyes
refusing to meet mine.
Doug, divorced from
your second wife,
your second three
children, no visitation
rights again; you are
unfit to love.

Lise, the terror
of small arms, muscles
never strong enough.
Every man I've known
could hold my hands
in his palms.
I could rest my raised
head on his chest.
Each time we wrestled
I'd play, fight, as hard
as I could, my fingers
pulsed red, every fiber
of muscle in my arms
quickened.
Every time he pinned me—
effortlessly. I swallowed
the emotions I wouldn't let
out of my throat
and trusted him.

He trusted me,
but each night I clutched
full glasses of booze until
I couldn't move to fill them.
Each day he waited, hoped.
Each night he clutched
a pillow so close
to his face, screamed
until his lungs
stopped, his eyes shut,
his fingers loosened
to the dark.

IV

The waves are not
too rough today.
I walk out
urged further by
the gentle tightening
of his hand. He tells me
jump with the waves,
and lifts me, almost
lets me ride.
My legs loosen
as they lift ever
so slightly off
the ground.
My smile surprises me
as my eyes open wide
in a splash of clear blue.

I could learn to float
in time, I feel. Maybe . . .
not such a long time.

Years Later

At a crib in a room
of blue and red clowns
I cried for the crib
cornered in my parents'
gray-chipped bedroom.
Their arms wanted
to rock out the world,
but in their arms
I felt a world
without primary colors.

You did not mean
to catch me crying,
but you pressed your hands
to the spaces in my back.
Your shirt absorbed my tears.

I do not know
if your arms felt
the tension
of cracked plaster,
but your arms have lulled
that world to sleep
for now.

The Pilgrim

I did not think the trip would take so long,
that waves would spike like icicles,
that salted air would chill to the heart itself,
that my legs would ache from gripping
        a rocking floor.

And worse, the sickness, the pain, the friends
convulsing in violent fevers, begging me not to leave
as silently I begged them   *Don't give up.*
As alone I whispered prayers
I knew no one would answer.

One by one they shriveled into hollow sacks of skin.
I stood by digging my fingers into a ratted shawl
while their emptied bodies were tossed to the sea.
I have inhaled them like sea air.
They will never fade from my memory.

. . . I used to feel the dream sustain me,
could close my eyes, run my fingertips
over the stone contours
of the City on the Hill;
I could clench hope in my fist.
But here in this wild place
where my eyes scrape against the bark
        of strange trees
where the smell of sap and thick green
        sticks in my throat,
I feel the blood of wind-chapped hands
look at the reflection of sunken cheeks,
eyes permanently sunk in black.
I clutch my arms around myself,
I cannot feel the same substance.
I close my eyes, try to hear
the click of feet on cobblestone streets:
There is nothing, no one.

Talking to a Woman in My Family

There are people who need no more
than to stretch their hands
for the milk across the table,
brush the bangs from a coughing child's face
bounce a dry bottom on their knees.

I sit with her, chin poised
in my hands, foot tapping
out the conference paper.
I am already on the plane.
She tries to converse
but my language is
the language of air.
I cannot translate it
or decipher her child's coos.

Does she wonder about me?
A woman staring into vacant
       space
planning a life of reworked papers
without the time (it must be time)
to feel a child's warmth
filling my arms.

The Madonna

I wanted a different kind of life . . .
the quiet of the morning sky
when I could rub my eyes,
wait for my thoughts, fill
the hours with meditation
on what they call God
and what I can explain only
as that which nourishes me,
completes me so that I am, well,
not God, but the most human I can be.

Then your messenger came, told me
of your choice.
What was I to say?

It's not that I regret having Jesus.
No, after the exhaustion of labor
I saw him, tiny enough to balance
in one arm, but a complete
person, stretching out perfectly
formed arms and legs,
crying out his own identity.
The life I alone had created
made me surge with joy.

But that little life took so much.
Before each dawn his screams pitched our home.
How could I give comfort when my body still
ached from lifting him through yesterday?
Without the chance to watch
the clouds configure, listen
to your own unimitated footsteps,
your mind is the summer earth
caking below your feet.

And such a willful child!
At only twelve he snuck away
to talk with the priests.
My child, his words steamed
what I remembered as my brain's fire.
Yet he saw me as the woman chosen
for the stable at Bethlehem:
"I must be about my father's business."

My words made flesh swept from town
to town, from one wary populace
to another.
Why are people so afraid
of living contemplation,
of teaching, sowing your thoughts?
If I had had the chance—
I know it could never be—
but if I'd had his chance
would they have feared me?

When they murdered him all I could do
was stand at his feet and cry
as he cried to you "Father
forgive them." As though
You had anything to forgive.

Revenge

It's easy to forgive
on a cross.

The red of your blood
thrashed out;
anger in puddles
under the sun;
arms nailed tautly open.
"Father, please help"
sounds like
"Father, forgive."

But wait
till strength bulges
in your thighs;
till you stand erect
above the crawling soldier
who gutted your side.
Till he cries to God
and you stand aloof
in power
in Heaven.

Casual Sex

"I want, I want, I want."
—Henderson the Rain King

I want to have casual sex.

I want to dress, feel my breasts under the silk I see
        coming off as I put it on.
I want to walk into a bar, pick my chair
        flick my eyes at the man I desire.

I want to be ushered into a cab,
talk about stupid things, hear some dumb lines,
see an apartment I don't have to clean or finance;
have him undress me, have him caress me, touch him,
feel nothing more resonant than muscles and curly hair.

And then—this is the best part—
since I'm a decade older, seasoned by academic tussles,
        marriage negotiations,
I'll know how to tell him what I like
        and we'll do it that way.

I want my diaphragm to protect me
from my husband's eyes that deepen with each
        friend's baby;
from the virus that squelches your immune system,
sucks the youth out of bodies, sucks the life
        out of friends;
from the publisher's deadlines, 9 am classes
that snip at foreplay, invade fantasies;
from the fantasies of the fourth decade
when your skin dries, your back aches;
from a decade of trying to secure, trying to achieve
        and the question—have you?

I want to have casual sex.

Death

Is it like the West?

The taste of sand
everywhere;
nowhere the sound
of voices you know.
Feet that pound concrete
twist on buttes
carved by water
sucked away
ages ago.

But maybe
with each step
your steps
are less strange.
The sun lulls your body
to its temperature,
tints your white flesh
to a beach brown.

And someone watches
as you sit down
resting on the landscape.

Good Friday Poetry

If I could have escaped the pain,
if I could have pushed the cup away,
smashed it down—I would have.
No question.

But I had no choice.
So I raised the cup, twisted it
in spring's evening air
pressed it to my lips
pressed it to yours.
This was my body, my blood.
This is my sacrament,
your sacrament.

Whenever you drink this wine
you may begin to think of me,
but as you sip again,
as the wine heats your pores,
as your thoughts mold to its spell—
what will you think of?

Can you taste cold, polished metal
and see reflections in gold?
Can it be that the passion is over?
That this perfect white and rounded host
        feels no pain . . .
Then what has become of me,
each time you swallow, what is it
        you absorb?
What is the body and blood when it
        is part of you?